CODE QUEST

HIEROGLYPHS

Written by Sean Callery

Illustrated by Jurgen Ziewe

KINGFISHER
LONDON & NEW YORK

Copyright © Kingfisher 2010
Published in the United States by Kingfisher,
175 Fifth Ave., New York, NY 10010
Kingfisher is an imprint of Macmillan Children's Books, London.
All rights reserved.

Distributed in the U.S. by Macmillan, 175 Fifth Ave.,
New York, NY 10010
Distributed in Canada by H.B. Fenn and Company Ltd.,
34 Nixon Road, Bolton, Ontario L7E 1W2

Library of Congress Cataloging-in-Publication data
has been applied for.

ISBN: 978-0-7534-6411-3

Kingfisher books are available for special promotions and
premiums. For details contact: Special Markets Department,
Macmillan, 175 Fifth Ave., New York, NY 10010.

For more information, please visit www.kingfisherpublications.com

Consultant: Margaret Maitland,
The Queen's College, University of Oxford
Additional illustrations: Peter Bull Art Studio
Concept and styling: Jo Connor
Narrative concept: Simon Holland
Special thanks to Winsome Malcolm for font creation

Printed in China
1 3 5 7 9 8 6 4 2
1TR/0210/LFG/UNTD/200SPCO/C

HOW TO USE THE CD

The CD contains an A–Z font (typeface) of hieroglyphic symbols, which can
be typed out using a standard computer keyboard. The font has been created
in different formats, to suit different computer operating systems: there is a
Mac Postscript font, a Mac TrueType font, a PC TrueType font, and an OpenType
font (for both Macs and PCs). For help or advice on installing fonts on your
computer, please consult your manual or use the Internet and search
for "installing fonts" for your specific operating system.

Disclaimer: Kingfisher excludes all liability for damage to hardware or loss of
data or profits arising from the use of, misuse of, or inability to use this
product, to the fullest extent permitted by applicable law.

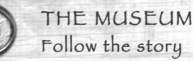

CONTENTS

MEET DR. STONE

I'm Dr. Cameron Stone, archaeologist. Prepare yourself. You are going to help me solve a mystery that is thousands of years old—and discover a new one.

Who is the mysterious character who shares my adventure?

Look out for the evidence in each exciting scene.

Cairo, Egypt
September 18

Dear Code Breaker,

My trip to Egypt was supposed to be a vacation, but it has ended up as quite an adventure. It began in a museum and led me to an undiscovered tomb. Along the way, I have had to break a lot of coded messages. I have kept them all, and you'll get a chance to solve them yourself in this book.

I'll never forget the Golden Cat or the strange guide who helped me find it.

Here is your challenge: read my story and look at all the clues and evidence I found. Can you break the codes, read the ancient writing, and solve the mystery along with me?

Even the smallest detail could reveal a vital clue!

HOW TO USE THIS BOOK

As you read through the book, you will see exciting scenes from my adventure. These are followed by "code-breaker" pages, in which I set out all of the clues for you to study. Evidence panels, such as the one on the right, will show you the key codes in the story and tell you what you need to do to crack them.

I'll show you how to translate the hieroglyphs in the clues.

CODE TWO: THE SCROLL

The letters didn't make familiar words because there were no vowels. But I experimented to find ways of dividing them up and adding vowels, to make the letters into recognizable words. Can you add the right vowels and complete the sentence?

w/cn/fnd/th/gldn/ct/tgthr/mt/m/n/th/msm/grdn

w/cn/fnd/th/
gldn/ct/tgthr/
mt/m/n/th/
msm/grdn

HIEROGLYPHIC CLUES

Don't let these symbols scare you! I will give you hints and tips to help you translate the ancient Egyptian symbols into familiar English. You will learn more as you go along.

THE CHARTS

Sometimes there will be a fold-out chart summarizing all the information you'll need to translate the symbols.

A–Z DECODER

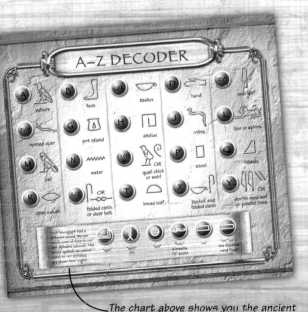

The chart above shows you the ancient Egyptian symbols that match up with sounds in today's A–Z alphabet.

THE SOLUTIONS

If you get stuck on a task, take a look at page 48, where all the answers are given and explained.

But no cheating! The harder you try to solve them yourself, the more you will learn about ancient Egyptian hieroglyphs.

THE HIEROGLYPHS CD

When you have reached the end of the story and want to use all the knowledge you have gathered, a CD will help you write your own words and messages in ancient Egyptian hieroglyphs. See pages 44–45 for full guidance on how to use it.

Our story is set in the present day, in the African land of Egypt. But it is all about the people who lived here thousands of years ago and the clues they left behind.

ANCIENT EGYPT

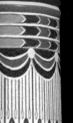

A giant statue of the pharaoh Rameses the Great on his throne

THE FERTILE NILE

The ancient Egyptian civilization lasted for 3,000 years. People began living in this part of Africa because they could grow plenty of food in the rich soil on either side of the Nile River. Beyond this was desert.

The Nile River

HALF-GODS

The rulers of the Egyptian kingdoms were called pharaohs. They were said to be half-human, half-god. They had complete power and were able to use their people as a workforce to build pyramids and tombs.

Mediterranean Sea

Alexandria

Nile Delta

Bubastis
Heliopolis
Giza • Memphis
Saqqara

FAYUM

LOWER EGYPT

Red Sea

SINAI

Heracleopolis

The pyramids at Giza

Eastern Desert

el-Amarna

Nile River

Dendera

Abydos

Valley of the Kings

Thebes

Hierakonpolis
Edfu

Western Desert

UPPER EGYPT

Elephantine

AFRICA

Nubian Desert

NUBIA

Valley of the Kings

GREAT ACHIEVEMENTS

The ancient Egyptians created a highly successful civilization, which we have learned about by looking at the art and objects they left behind.

Their civilization lasted thousands of years—from 3150 to 31 B.C. Today, we can see evidence of their achievements.

They were very good farmers.

They found ways to take water from the Nile River to help their crops grow.

They had a powerful army.

They built pyramids, tombs, and temples.

They developed paper and a system of writing.

Hieroglyphs in the Book of the Dead papyrus scroll (left)

HIEROGLYPHS

We know a lot about the ancient Egyptians because they had writing. It is called hieroglyphs ("sacred carving")—a set of pictures used as signs. These form an "alphabet" of about 1,000 symbols, each with at least one meaning or sound.

Hieroglyphic symbols carved into stone (below)

WALL INSCRIPTIONS

Hieroglyphs were written on walls in paintings and carvings (above), on objects such as pottery, and on paper. The paper was called papyrus and was made from the reeds that grew by the Nile River. Some ancient sheets of papyrus have lasted to the present day.

A wall painting from the tomb of a scribe named Menna (above)

SCRIBES

During ancient Egyptian times, only about one in a hundred people could read or write. They were known as scribes. If you wanted to send a message, you paid a scribe to write it for you. This wall painting (above) shows a scribe who served the pharaoh Tuthmosis IV.

RIDDLE WRITING

Hieroglyphs were used all through the ancient Egyptian period. They were in use for more years than the modern alphabet has even existed! But after they died out, nobody was able to read them for 1,200 years. Their meaning was finally revealed in the 1800s (see pages 42–43).

An excavator studies writing inside a governor's tomb in Bawiti, Egypt.

The Egyptians loved life but felt it was too short. They believed that their spirit could live forever if it was helped into the afterlife, the "new world" after death.

LIFE AFTER DEATH

The mummified body of Pharaoh (King) Tuthmosis IV

Facial features are still visible.

The arms are crossed over the chest to show that he is royal.

Linen bandages

The body's internal organs were stored in Canopic jars such as these.

MUMMIFICATION
To the Egyptians, preserving a dead body was a way of keeping its spirit alive. They would wash it and remove the major organs. The brain was taken out though the nostrils with a metal hook and thrown away. Then the body was dried with natron, a kind of salt. Finally, it was stuffed to the right shape and wrapped in linen.

A SET OF COFFINS
After mummification, the body was placed in a wooden box or coffin, which was then put inside a large stone container called a sarcophagus. The coffin was decorated with protective spells. A death mask showed the person's face so that their spirit could recognize them. Sometimes two coffins were used, one inside the other (right).

Base of inner coffin

"Body mask" to cover mummy

The lids of the coffins were often decorated with hieroglyphs. These might include magic spells to frighten robbers or to help the dead person enter the afterlife.

Hieroglyphs in bandage-like strips

Lid of inner coffin

Objects were put in the tomb to help with life in the next world. These could include gold, silver, and valuable jewels, as well as "mummified" food and drink. There were also doll-like figures, called shabtis, that would become servants in the afterlife.

Such treasures also included models of things that the person owned in the real world, which the Egyptians believed they could take with them and use in the world to come.

A wooden shabti figure, painted in bright colors

A model of a boat, with its owner sitting inside the covered cabin

PIT BURIALS

At first, only pharaohs were preserved and protected in death. Then their families were included. Later, anyone who could afford it was mummified and entombed. Poorer people were buried in the desert where the dry sand sometimes preserved their bodies (right).

This is a reconstruction of a shallow grave pit, where this man was buried more than 5,000 years ago.

Lid of outer coffin

THE MUSEUM

Right after breakfast, I hurried to my favorite museum. That's how a top-notch archaeologist likes to start a vacation! Some guides were chatting on the street, waiting for the first groups of the day.

"It's our friend Dr. Stone, the famous archaeologist!" one called out. "You know more about ancient Egypt than we do . . . Take us on a tour!"

I was still laughing when a woman bumped into me. As I stumbled and fell, I caught sight of a green scarf held in place by a golden, cat-shaped brooch.

"Hey, be careful!" I called. But she had vanished . . . into the museum?

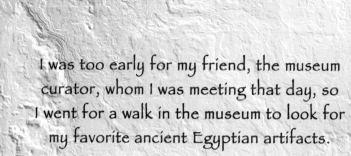

I was too early for my friend, the museum curator, whom I was meeting that day, so I went for a walk in the museum to look for my favorite ancient Egyptian artifacts.

But somehow I took a wrong turn and got completely lost.

"Maybe I need a guide after all," I said to myself as I pushed open a heavy door and found myself in a dark room I'd never seen before. It was very gloomy in there because the windows were hidden by curtains—all except one at the back of the room.

The air felt damp, and I had a strange feeling that I was being watched. But there was nobody around.

The door blew shut behind me.

What was going on?

THE GOLDEN CAT

In front of me was a beautiful golden statue of a cat, sitting up on its haunches. It looked proud and elegant. Why had I never seen it before? Where was it from? I tried to read its label but the ink had run. A gust of wind made the hair on my neck stand up. Suddenly, I was freezing cold. This was getting creepy.

I headed for the door but a sound like a whisper made me turn back. Had that scroll of paper behind the cat's paws been there all the time? As I picked up the scroll, I looked into the cat's sparkling eyes. Did it blink? I could almost make out the figure of a person in those blue gems . . . No. It must have been the reflection of the curtains behind me, still fluttering from that gust of wind. I had to get out of there. I grabbed the label and the scroll, and ran.

I studied the label and the scroll. At first, they didn't make sense. Then I figured them out, and I knew I wasn't on vacation anymore. I had a mission to find something.

A MESSAGE

All the artifacts in the room had handwritten paper labels on them, as if they had recently been delivered to the museum.

wallpaintingsin
thetombshow
twogoldencats
butonlyonestatue
wasfound

NO PUNCTUATION!
Just like the smudged label on the cat statue, ancient Egyptian hieroglyphs had no capital letters, periods, or even spaces between words. This is something to keep in mind when looking at the clues and translating the hieroglyphic inscriptions in this book.

This model (below) shows Egyptian workers making bread and beer.

CODE ONE: THE LABEL
The label had become wet and smudged in the damp air so that the words were all blended together, with no punctuation. This made it hard to read. Can you figure out what it says?

wallpaintingsinthetombshowtwo
goldencatsbutonlyonestatuewasfound

Here are some of my favorite objects in the museum. I saw them before I came across the cat.

A gold collar, inlaid with colored glass and semiprecious stones

The scroll I found underneath the cat had lots of tiny symbols on it, all crowded together. Eventually, I could see that they were letters. When I figured out what they said, I realized I would have some help on my mission.

This is the scroll I found tucked underneath the statue of the cat. Was it a message?

CODE TWO: THE SCROLL

The letters didn't make familiar words because there were no vowels. But I experimented to find ways of dividing them up and adding vowels, to make the letters into recognizable words. Can you add the right vowels and complete the sentence?

w/cn/fnd/th/gldn/ct/tgthr/
mt/m/n/th/msm/grdn

w/cn/fnd/th/
gldn/ct/tgthr/
mt/m/n/th/
msm/grdn

NO VOWELS!

The Egyptians did not include vowels—the letters a, e, i, o, and u—in their writing. However, when we are trying to understand their picture writing, there are certain symbols that we can interpret as the "vowel sounds" of our alphabet, which are as follows:

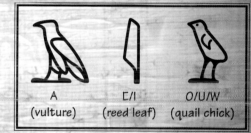

| A (vulture) | E/I (reed leaf) | O/U/W (quail chick) |

Hawk's head decoration at each end

Our A–Z of letters is known as the "Roman" alphabet. The ancient Egyptians had hieroglyphs for certain sounds that do not exist in the Roman alphabet. These symbols are shown here (right).

You may come across these symbols in this book, but they will not appear in the words and clues that you have to decode.

"ayin"   "aych" (H)   "tch"

"huh," a breathy "H" sound   "sh"   "ch," as in the Scottish word "loch"

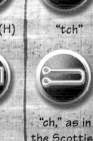

15

The Egyptians believed that some gods appeared as animals. So various creatures, especially cats, were regarded as holy. They were protected and worshiped.

CAT WORSHIP

The name "Horus" means "He Who Is Above."

Cat shaped out of a gemstone called chalcedony

Gold ring with a cat decoration

Horus wears the crown of all Egypt.

CATS EVERYWHERE
Cat statues were displayed in temples and put inside houses for protection. Cat designs were popular on jewelry, too. Children were often called by the nickname "Miu" or "Miut," the old Egyptian word for cat, which sounds like the animal's "meow" noise.

ANIMAL WORSHIP
Animals of every kind were respected and revered by the ancient Egyptians. They were thought to be in close contact with gods that the average Egyptian could not reach. Horus (left), a god of the sky, was usually depicted as a falcon or as a man with a falcon's head.

USEFUL CATS
Cats killed mice and other pests that ate grain in storage places, as well as dangerous snakes, so farmers tamed them and put them to work. Cats were kept in the home and made good pets, as they do today. They were also taken on hunting trips to bring back the dead prey. This tomb painting (above) shows a cat stalking birds.

Bronze statue of the goddess Bastet

When a cat died, its owners would mourn it as if it were a person. The body would be dried and mummified and then placed in a cat-shaped coffin of wood, bronze, or clay. This painted, wooden cat sarcophagus (left) is from about 330–305 B.C.

To mummify a cat, the Egyptians dried its body naturally. The internal organs were removed and the body stuffed with sand or packing material. The body was then put in a sitting position and wrapped in linen bandages (above). A face and other designs were added in black ink.

A CAT GOD

The goddess Bastet, daughter of the sun god Ra or Re, appeared either as a cat or as a woman with a cat's head. All the gods had jobs, and Bastet's was to protect women, children, and, of course, cats. She was also identified with music and dance. Bastet could be both gentle and fierce—like a cat.

CAT CITY

A cat religion was based around the city of Bubastis, where a special festival was held every year. Hundreds of thousands of mummified cats have been found in underground cemeteries here. There were even "cat farms" for breeding cats to be sacrificed to the gods.

This picture (above) shows broken columns at the ruined Temple of Bastet, in the Egyptian Delta region, where the city of Bubastis once stood.

17

MEET NEFRET

Someone was waiting for me in the museum garden. It was the woman who had knocked me over outside. "I am Nefret. I can help you find the missing cat." How did she know I had decided to search for it?

"I will be your guide. We will start at the tomb where the golden cat was found." "Why do you need me?" I asked. "You are an archaeologist. They'll let you into the tombs," she replied.

We rode to the site on donkeys, and by noon we'd reached the entrance to our tomb. When we got down to the main burial chamber, we saw there was a small hole in the rock just big enough for someone to squeeze through. "That must be how the robbers got in," said Nefret, "so we can do the same."

I almost bumped into the huge stone coffin. Nefret showed me the pharaoh's name written on the lid inside a curved line. "It's a cartouche," I said. "That means it's a royal name."

I kicked something on the sandy floor. It was a piece of pottery with writing on it. Nefret stared at it in amazement. "There is a name on this, too," she said.

TWO NAMES

A ROYAL NAME
Royal names were written inside an oval shape called a cartouche. The shieldlike emblem looked like a loop of rope and signified eternity, which means "forever." The letter sounds of the name were not always written in the right order. The scribe would often swap them around to make a nicer shape.

It looked to me as if the scribe had switched the last two hieroglyphs . . .

Tomb entrance

First corridor

Our plan of the tomb

Stairwell

Second corridor

First hall

Stairwell

The missing cat may have been taken from the main burial chamber or from an annex (a storeroom). My hunch is that the two cats originally stood in the same room as the pharaoh's sarcophagus.

Annex

Annex

Annex

Main burial chamber

Annex

Sarcophagus (large coffin)

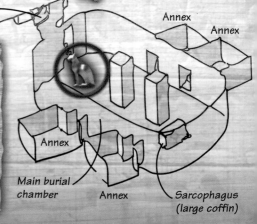

CODE THREE: THE CARTOUCHE

To help you find whose tomb it is, I have put the hieroglyphs from the cartouche in order, left to right. The first symbol has two possible sounds, but they are very similar. I have added two vowel sounds in red. If they have more than one sound, you'll just have to guess!

20

A CLUE IN PIECES

Fragments of broken pottery lay all over the floor of the main chamber. When I showed Nefret the piece I had tripped over, she got very excited. "There is the name of a man," she said, "and he is asking the gods to forgive him. He could be the tomb robber!"

CODE FOUR: THE BROKEN POTTERY

The message on the pottery was very short. I translated the words, "Show mercy to me . . . ," and this was followed by a name. You can use the A–Z chart under the flap (right) to decode the robber's name. I have added a vowel sound in red.

This piece of broken pottery has symbols on it that make up a name.

Nefret studied the broken fragments carefully, squinting her eyes. Would this name lead us to the missing cat?

CODE BREAKER

THE WORKERS' VILLAGE

We met again at dawn the next day. "I know a place where we might find out about Deduhapy," said Nefret as she climbed onto her donkey. On our way, Nefret told me that the ancient tomb workers—mostly skilled craftsmen and painters—lived in a place known as the Workers' Village, close to the tombs of the Valley of the Kings. "They knew where the secret tombs were and what was inside them," she said. "Sometimes they went back and robbed them. Maybe that's what happened to the second cat."

A group had gathered near one of the buildings. "Hey, there's a dig going on," said Nefret. "That's the foreman's house. Ask them what they've found." So I did, and once the diggers knew I was an archaeologist, they showed me some sheets of ancient papyrus. It was a list of the workers who built Sematawy's tomb.

Deduhapy was one of the last names on the list. He was one of the painters who decorated the inside of the tomb.

Then I noticed something. "Why is there a bird next to his name?" I asked.

"It's a sparrow. That symbol has a special meaning. If it was written next to his name, it means he did something bad!" said Nefret. "He must be the tomb robber!"

"But if Deduhapy was caught, the things he stole would have been put back," I said. "And we know that one of the golden cats was never returned to the tomb."

"Whoever captured Deduhapy must have kept the other cat," replied Nefret. "They even wrote his name on the broken piece of pottery you found, so he would get all the blame."

Suddenly, Nefret's green eyes blazed. "I know—I bet his boss betrayed him and took the statue for himself."

We went back to the museum to look for letters from Heruher to the new pharaoh. The curator brought us the documents we were looking for.

BETRAYED!

Nefret was intrigued by the name "Heruher."

When I read the letters, I knew we had discovered the real thief—Heruher. He had put only one of the cats back in Sematawy's tomb. But where was the one he had kept?

I translated Heruher's letters and copied the most important messages into my notebook.

ANOTHER PHARAOH
Look at Code Five on the opposite page. It reveals the person Heruher was writing to. Can you figure out his name? It was the hardest code to crack, but it took us another step closer to finding the missing cat.

May the Gods help you rule us wisely for many years. Sematawy's tomb has been robbed. I caught the robbers myself and will bring them to the palace. You can decide how they are to be punished. They took a lot of treasure. I have put it all back in the tomb.

I have many gold and silver gifts for you and your daughter, whom I like very much.

I long to be your faithful servant.

Heruher

A god's name was often added to a pharaoh's title. The name of the god that appears in this cartouche (right) is the sun god, Re: ⊙

• The god's name always came first in a cartouche, even if it came later in the spoken name. In this case, it is spoken at the end. The rest of the symbols are in the right order, and they begin with the "W" sound. I've put in one vowel sound to help you. You will need to add one more vowel. Try saying the name out loud when you have identified the correct sounds.

• The full name of a pharaoh usually said something about the god. This name means "The justice of Re is great."

Amun, the king of the gods—later combined with Ra as the god Amun-Ra.

Example name (right): TutankhAMUN (18th-dynasty pharaoh)

Here are examples of gods' names appearing in real cartouches:

 Re or Ra, the sun god

Example name (above): MenkauRE (builder of the third pyramid at Giza)

 Seth, god of chaos, storms, and the desert

Example name (above): SETy Merneptah (father of Rameses the Great)

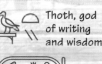 Thoth, god of writing and wisdom

Example name (above): THUTmosis III (18th-dynasty pharaoh and empire builder)

 Sobek, a crocodile god of the Nile and protector of the king

Example name (above): SOBEKhotep (13th-dynasty pharaoh)

 Horus, the god of kingship (a pharaoh was thought to be a "living Horus")

Example name (above): MenkauHOR (5th-dynasty pharaoh)

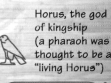

ANOTHER TOMB

It seemed that Heruher had bribed his way to get close to the pharaoh, Wermatre. We hoped that the golden cat was one of Heruher's gifts to the pharaoh and would be in his tomb, our next destination.

Inside Wermatre's main burial chamber, pictures and carvings on the wall showed glorious events from his rule.

The pharaoh had fought great battles to protect Egypt and to take more land. Wermatre himself had ridden in a chariot and given orders during a battle. There were pictures showing how he had told archers to fire arrows at enemy boats on the sea.

The enemy leader's body was hung upside down on the front of Wermatre's ship as he sailed home to Egypt.

The inscriptions we found showed how Wermatre had punished the robbers who had stolen from Sematawy's tomb.

Tomb entrance

PUNISHED!

In the tomb, there was also a list of Wermatre's most trusted friends. Heruher was near the top. His bribe had worked . . . The inscriptions showed that he married the pharaoh's daughter and became his official seal bearer.

The tomb paintings showed robbers being put on trial and beaten for their crimes.

The inscriptions that interested us the most were in the corner of the main burial chamber.

LAW AND ORDER
Justice was represented by Ma'at, the goddess of world order (right). The pharaohs, as living gods, were the people who controlled trials and judgments over those who committed crimes.

CODE SIX: OUCH!
Wermatre was clearly a king who believed in the importance of law and justice. His tomb was decorated with pictures showing how he had punished criminals. This one (left) is about what was done to Deduhapy and shows a large pile of hands. What do you think happened to him?

I tried to copy down as many inscriptions as I could find, showing the ways in which criminals were punished under the rule of Wermatre. What kind of punishments do you think these pictures show?

A SIGN OF OWNERSHIP

This is an ancient Egyptian bronze branding iron. It was heated over a fire and used to burn a symbol into the hides of cattle so people would know whom they belonged to. But how do you think branding irons were related to justice and punishment?

A ROYAL SEAL BEARER

Seals were used for a number of things: to mark ownership, to "lock" important documents, rooms, or objects, and to act as a "signature." A royal seal bearer (right) had the power to make things happen in the king's name and could use the royal seal to authorize commands.

Ma'at, normally shown with her wings outstretched, represented truth, order, and cosmic balance.

But there was no golden cat here.

"It must be in Heruher's tomb," said Nefret, tapping her long nails together, "and we don't know where that is."

We had to go back to the museum and hunt for more clues.

The famous Egyptian pyramids were glorious tombs for pharaohs, their families, and officials. All of them were robbed of their valuables.

TOMB RAIDERS

PYRAMIDS AND TOMBS

Because of all the robberies, the Egyptian kings abandoned building pyramids and instead cut tombs out of solid rock. Many of these tombs were in the isolated Valley of the Kings. The valley was near a pyramid-shaped mountain and could be protected by guards more easily.

Under cover of darkness, robbers approach the Great Pyramid of Giza, which contains the burial chamber of the pharaoh (king) Khufu.

This is the entrance to a tomb in the Valley of the Kings (above).

A BOY KING'S TOMB

Every royal tomb we know of was robbed, often by the very people who had built it. There is one exception, where priests caught the robbers and put the treasure back. This was the tomb of Tutankhamun, discovered again in 1922. It was filled with hundreds of valuables, as well as the body of the boy pharaoh himself.

This reconstruction of an antechamber inside Tutankhamun's tomb shows the amount of treasure provided for the afterlife.

Archaeologist Howard Carter inspects Tutankhamun's coffin (above left).

Once finished, a tomb's entrance would be sealed, plastered over, and hidden under rocks. The builders tried to deter or confuse robbers by adding false passages leading nowhere, hidden doors that looked like part of the wall, corridors that changed direction, and sliding gates.

Curses warning robbers to stay away were sometimes written at the entrance. These included "he shall be cooked"; "his arm will be cut off and his neck twisted off like a bird's"; and "he shall die of hunger and thirst."

A curse inside this doorway reads, "Those who enter will be eaten by crocodiles and snakes."

DARK AND DANGEROUS

It was pitch black inside the tombs. Raiders could only see what their candles lit up as they crept along the tunnels. They carried lucky charms known as amulets to protect against spells. Sometimes robbers would set fire to the wooden coffins. Later, they would return to take away the precious melted metals inside.

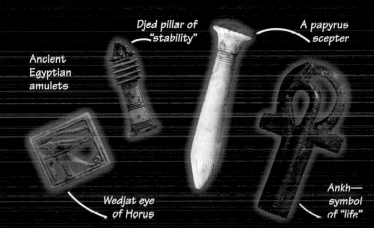

Djed pillar of "stability"

A papyrus scepter

Ancient Egyptian amulets

Wedjat eye of Horus

Ankh— symbol of "life"

ANOTHER MESSAGE

Back at the museum, I found the curator and told him what we had found. As soon as I said Heruher's name, his eyes lit up and he showed me an exhibit. "I just found this bowl in a storeroom. It has a message to Heruher in the afterlife from his wife."

Faster than a panther, Nefret grabbed the bowl and studied the writing on its inside. She whispered in my ear: "It mentions a gift that she left for him in his tomb."

"But we don't know where he was buried," I muttered. "Why don't we ask the curator?"

"No!" she hissed. "These pictures tell us where to go." She seized a pen and paper and copied the symbols.

"Catch!" cried Nefret, throwing the bowl high into the air. As the curator dived to stop it from smashing to the floor, Nefret ran toward the exit. "Hurry!" she called, "We've got to get there first!"

As I ran alongside her, Nefret handed me the translations she had scribbled down. I was too out of breath to ask where we were going.

ODD DIRECTIONS

A letter from Hemira to her dearest husband Heruher. I hope you were happy with your funeral and that you like the special gift in your tomb. I know you are among friends. Watch over me until I may join you again in the afterlife.

First of all, I checked Nefret's translation of the symbols inside the bowl. It is shown here (left), scribbled on the museum notepaper. I could not believe my eyes—it really was a message from Heruher's wife. Her name was Hemira, and we knew this to be the name of Wermatre's daughter.

Letters to the dead were written by relatives of the deceased, generally asking for their help. The spirits of the dead were believed to be very powerful. The message on this offerings bowl (below right) was from a mother to her dead son.

Messages to the dead were often written on bowls, which could also be filled with offerings of food or drink to the spirit of the deceased.

IDEOGRAMS
Some hieroglyphs are "ideograms." These are like picture writing, showing an idea or a place. For example, today we draw a heart shape to mean "love." Some objects were shaped like ideograms. This amulet (far right) is in the shape of the "ankh" sign, which represented "life" and the action of living.

This amulet was intended to protect the dead in the afterlife.

The ideograms on the bowl were not part of the main message. They seemed to be giving us some sort of clue—perhaps the most important one so far!

CODE SEVEN: THE IDEOGRAMS

Above are the ideogram picture symbols from the edge of the bowl that Nefret had noted down in the museum. They seemed to be giving directions to somewhere. Could it be another tomb? Try to decode the ideograms using the fold-out guide on the right to find out where Nefret was taking me.

IDEOGRAMS

You might expect an Egyptian tomb to be plain and dark because we often connect dark colors with death, but Egyptian tombs were full of color.

TOMB TALES

ENTRY TO THE NEXT WORLD

In ancient Egypt, people thought dying was just another part of their journey, not its end. It was very important for the dead person's name to be displayed in the tomb so that their spirit lived on. Otherwise, they might not get into the afterlife successfully.

A HEAVENLY IMAGE

The decorations in a royal tomb were all from books about the afterlife. But officials' tombs included pictures from their lives and images of what they wanted in the next world. The painting below is from the tomb of a senior scribe named Nebamun and shows him hunting on the Nile, standing above his daughter and in front of his wife.

MAGIC PASSWORDS

Tomb inscriptions included spells and passwords to assist the dead person's journey into the next world. Inside the pyramid of Unas at Saqqara (above), spells cover the walls and ceiling of the burial chamber.

Can you spot the duck, fish . . . and a cat? The cat's eye in the painting is made of real gold.

This scene from a stele (engraved stone monument) shows a nobleman and his wife being given offerings by family members.

TOMB SUPPLIES

There were drawings of food, drink, and other supplies that would help in the afterlife. These were also represented by models—some survive of little bakeries and farms, and boats to help in the journey. These models (below) show a procession of offering-bearers, bringing supplies into the tomb.

BIG MEANS IMPORTANT

The more important you were, the bigger you would be drawn in pictures. Parents are bigger than their children (above), and servants are often tiny while the pharaoh is enormous. Wives are usually shown as slightly smaller than their husband—but if they loved each other a lot, they might be shown equal in size (right).

These painted limestone statues are of Prince Rahotep, high priest of Heliopolis, and his wife Nofret.

The models were made out of wood and then painted.

To create a tomb picture, the artist would first draw a design on a board with a grid on it. A much larger grid was painted in red on the white walls of the tomb. Using the smaller grid on the board as a guide, the outlines of the design were painted in black ink—or carved with a chisel—on the large wall grid. Once the whole image was in place on the wall, the black outlines were filled in with bright colors. The artist then finished off his work.

The small squares were used to get the size and shape of the body right.

A board sketch, from about 1450 B.C., of Pharaoh Thutmosis III. The artist also did practice drawings of hieroglyphs (top).

A HIDDEN TOMB

We used the clues to find our way, following a river to the north. Eventually, we came to an old, crumbling wall at the foot of a hill.

"But this is Wermatre's tomb. We've already searched here!" I panted. "Yes, but I think there is a hidden chamber," Nefret replied.

Nefret began to examine the four sides of the main burial chamber. She tapped along the walls with her long, sharp nails. As she moved along, the sound changed. Part of one wall was hollow. Nefret's bright green eyes glowed with excitement.

"Heruher married Wermatre's daughter," she explained. "So he joined the family." Now I got it. "And families were buried together . . . !" I exclaimed. "Exactly," said Nefret. "Their tomb is hidden behind this plaster panel."

When I kicked the wall, my boot went right through. We peered into the hole . . .

And there it was. The hidden tomb. Inside it were two large stone coffins—one for Heruher and one for his wife, Hemira.

FOUND!

At last—we had made our discovery.

Standing between them, staring right at us, was the golden cat. "Go on," Nefret said softly from behind me. "It wants to be picked up." I lifted the shining statue. It was smooth and heavy. I was surprised how warm it felt. "Here," I said, turning, "you hold it."

But she wasn't there.

I returned to the museum, but she was nowhere to be seen. The curator we spoke to said he'd never seen Nefret until that day.

"Nefret is an old name," he said. "Nobody is called that these days."

When we put the golden cats next to each other at the museum, it felt as if the room was filling with light. The cats were smiling.

Just like its partner, the cat we found in Heruher's tomb had gems in its eyes. But they were a different color.

I had seen eyes like that before . . .

They were bright green.

What was Nefret's true identity?

CODE EIGHT: WHO WAS NEFRET?
On page 48, you will find all of the answers to the Code Quest challenges in this story. Did you get them all right? Good job.
Together, we have solved the Mystery of the Golden Cat.
But what about Nefret? Did you figure out who she was?

LET'S HAVE A LOOK AT THE CLUES . . .
• She did not talk to the other guides and curators. She would only talk to me, because I could help her find the tombs.
• Nefret had long, sharp fingernails—like a cat's claws.
• She had amazingly bright, emerald-green eyes. Just like the Golden Cat's.
• She wore a bright green headscarf and a golden brooch.
• The name "Nefret" is an ancient Egyptian name. It means "beautiful."

NEFRET: WHAT'S IN A NAME?

So, how would you express the name "Nefret" ("beautiful") in ancient Egyptian hieroglyphs?

To the right, I have set out the symbols of her name in a way that describes her perfectly.

This is a "triliteral," or three-letter symbol, which shows that the word starts with the sound "nfr" (see page 44).

The "n" symbol.

The "f" symbol.

The "r" symbol.

The "t" symbol. Using this at the end of the word makes the word feminine (female).

This is a "determinative" symbol, used to describe Nefret as a cat, or "feline" (see pages 44–45).

And this is another type of determinative sign, to show that Nefret was female.

People and animal signs give you the clue you need to read them in the right direction. You read "into the face" of these symbols—so here, you should read the name from left to right. For the Egyptians, the normal direction of reading was right to left, but they also wrote left to right and top to bottom.

For more than a thousand years, nobody was able to read hieroglyphic writing. The key to unlocking its secrets was the Rosetta Stone.

CODE STONE

THE DISCOVERY

The Rosetta Stone is the most famous slab of rock in the history of archaeology. It is 46 in. (118cm) high, 30 in. (77cm) across, and weighs over three-fourths of a ton. It was found in 1799 by French soldiers who were knocking down a wall in the village of Rosetta, Egypt. It was taken by the British army in 1801 and is displayed in the British Museum in London, England.

Top section: written in hieroglyphs

Middle section: written in demotic script

Bottom section: written in ancient Greek

This one object was the key to deciphering hieroglyphs because the same words appear in three different languages. The top part is in Egyptian hieroglyphs. The middle is in demotic, a later version of hieroglyphs used for more everyday writing. The bottom section is in classic Greek, a language that some scholars still understood.

The stone's translators realized that they could use their knowledge of ancient Greek to figure out what the hieroglyphs said. They also used their knowledge of the Coptic language, a more modern Egyptian language that had evolved from the ancient Egyptian version. From this single text, they discovered the alphabet of sounds and other symbols of an ancient, lost method of communication.

THE TRANSLATORS

The first breakthrough was made by an Englishman named Thomas Young (left). He realized that the hieroglyphs stood for sounds, not letters, and was able to find the name of the pharaoh ruling when the writing was done: Ptolemy. But Young stopped his work, and the major advances were achieved by a Frenchman, Jean-François Champollion (right), from 1822 to 1824.

Thomas Young
(1773–1829)

Jean-François Champollion
(1790–1832)

A notebook belonging to Jean-François Champollion, showing illustrations of hieroglyphs (below)

THE BREAKTHROUGH

Champollion used Young's technique on some other Egyptian cartouches, including one that ended with a repeated symbol. He guessed that the first hieroglyph, shaped like a disk, represented the sun, which he knew could be spoken as "ra."

So, now his translation was "ra-?-s-s," and he recognized the name of a famous pharaoh: Rameses the Great (Rameses II). The ancient code was broken at last.

1   The canal symbol: "Mri"
    (meaning "beloved")

2   The god Amun symbol

3   Sun god symbol: "Ra"

4   The fox skins symbol: "MS"
    (meaning "born of")

5   Folded cloth symbol: "S"

6   Folded cloth symbol: "S"

This is an ancient Egyptian wall painting of Rameses II dressed for war, from about 1184 to 1153 B.C.

The cartouche of Rameses II, also known as Rameses the Great

43

All the hieroglyph words and names used on these pages can be found in this book. You can also use the accompanying CD to write in hieroglyphs.

CODE MAKER

MAKING DIFFERENT SOUNDS
If the letter alphabet on page 21 was all you needed to write hieroglyphs, it would be easy! But there were about 800 hieroglyph "letters." These included two-letter ("biliteral") sounds, three-letter ("triliteral") sounds, ideograms (see page 35), and other signs.

"AB" is an example of a biliteral sound sign, made up of two letters.

DECODING NAMES
As you already know, from reading page 16, cats and children were often known by the nickname "MIU," which is a triliteral (three-letter) sound. Here are the three symbols that form the cat sound:

EXTRA INFORMATION SIGNS
Special signs, called determinatives, are symbols that come at the end of a word to give you an idea of what type of word it is and what it means. They are a bit like a "picture summary" of the whole word.

Because determinatives always come at the end of a word, they can also be really useful in figuring out where a word finishes and a new one begins.

| man | woman | king | child | soldier |

| enemy | tired, weak | old | noble | cat, feline |

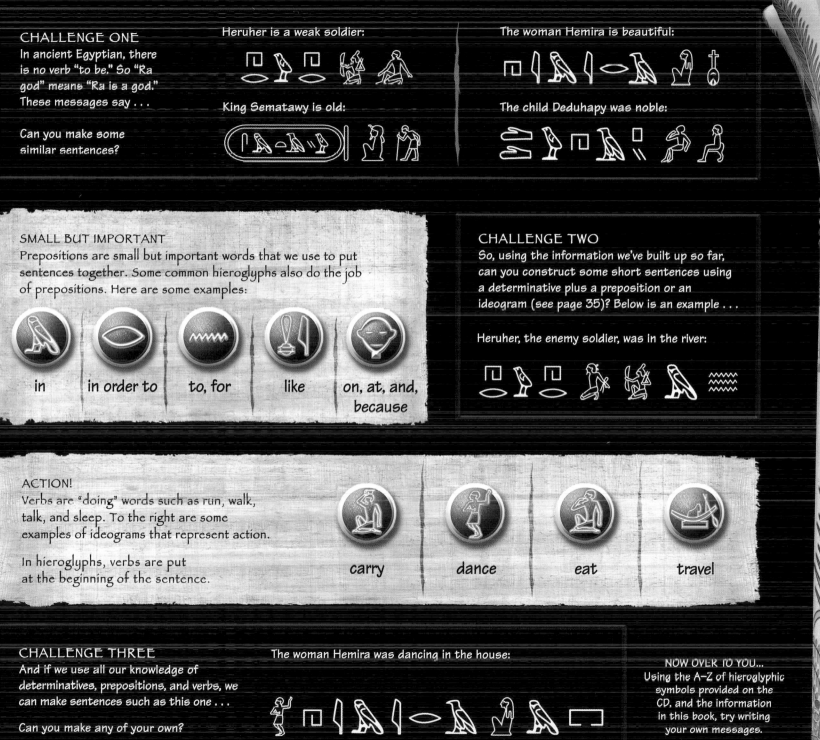

CHALLENGE ONE
In ancient Egyptian, there is no verb "to be." So "Ra god" means "Ra is a god." These messages say . . .

Can you make some similar sentences?

Heruher is a weak soldier:

King Sematawy is old:

The woman Hemira is beautiful:

The child Deduhapy was noble:

SMALL BUT IMPORTANT
Prepositions are small but important words that we use to put sentences together. Some common hieroglyphs also do the job of prepositions. Here are some examples:

in

in order to

to, for

like

on, at, and, because

CHALLENGE TWO
So, using the information we've built up so far, can you construct some short sentences using a determinative plus a preposition or an ideogram (see page 35)? Below is an example . . .

Heruher, the enemy soldier, was in the river:

ACTION!
Verbs are "doing" words such as run, walk, talk, and sleep. To the right are some examples of ideograms that represent action.

In hieroglyphs, verbs are put at the beginning of the sentence.

carry

dance

eat

travel

CHALLENGE THREE
And if we use all our knowledge of determinatives, prepositions, and verbs, we can make sentences such as this one . . .

Can you make any of your own?

The woman Hemira was dancing in the house:

NOW OVER TO YOU...
Using the A–Z of hieroglyphic symbols provided on the CD, and the information in this book, try writing your own messages.

INDEX

PICTURE CREDITS

The Publisher would like to thank the following for permission to reproduce their material. Every care has been taken to trace copyright holders. However, if there have been any unintentional omissions or failure to trace copyright holders, we apologize and will, if informed, endeavor to make corrections in any future edition.

(t = top, b = bottom, c = center, l = left, r = right):

Pages 6l Photolibrary/Bildagentur Rm; 6c Shutterstock/Ramzi Hachicho; 6tr Shutterstock/sculpies; 6br Shutterstock/Mirek Hejnicki; 7tl Shutterstock/modestlife; 7tc Art Archive/Musée du Louvre, Paris/Dagli Orti; 7tr Art Archive/Dagli Orti; 7c Shutterstock/Sergieiev; 7bc Reuters/STR New; 8l Corbis/Thomas Hartwell; 8c Art Archive/Musée du Louvre, Paris/Dagli Orti; 8–9 akg-images/Erich Lessing; 9tl Art Archive/Egyptian Museum, Turin/Dagli Orti; 9c Art Archive/Musée du Louvre, Paris/Dagli Orti; 9br With the Kind Permission of the Trustees of the British Museum, London; 14br Art Archive/Musée du Louvre, Paris/Dagli Orti; 15bl Art Archive/Egyptian Museum, Cairo/Dagli Orti; 16l Corbis/Gianni Dagli Orti; 16c With the Kind Permission of the Trustees of the British Museum; 16r Art Archive/Dagli Orti; 17l Art Archive/Musée du Louvre, Paris/Dagli Orti; 17tc Art Archive/Musée du Louvre, Paris/Dagli Orti; 17tr Art Archive/Musée du Louvre, Paris/Dagli Orti; 17bc Shutterstock/L. Quintanilla; 17br Alamy/Jim Henderson; 25 Shutterstock/Stefanie Leuker; 28cl Theban Mapping Project; 29l Alamy/Helene Rogers; 29tr With the Kind Permission of the Trustees of the British Museum; 29b Shutterstock/André Klaassen; 30 Photolibary; 30cr Shutterstock/Jakez; 31tl Getty/APIC; 31tr Art Archive/Pharaonic Village Cairo/Dagli Orti; 31c PA/AP/Ben Curtis; 31br Art Archive/Egyptian Museum, Turin/Dagli Orti; 34cr Art Archive/Musée du Louvre, Paris/Dagli Orti; 34br With the Kind Permission of the Trustees of the British Museum; 35 Shutterstock/Liudmila Gridina; 36l Art Archive/Dagli Orti; 36c Werner Forman Archive; 36br With the Kind Permission of the Trustees of the British Museum; 37tc Art Archive/Musée du Louvre, Paris/Dagli Orti; 37tr Art Archive/Egyptian Museum Cairo/Dagli Orti; 37bl Art Archive/Musée du Louvre, Paris/Dagli Orti; 42 With the Kind Permission of the Trustees of the British Museum; 43tl Alamy/The London Art Archive; 43tc Alamy/The London Art Archive; 43tr Alamy/The Print Collector; 43bl Corbis/The Gallery Collection.

THE MYSTERY OF THE GOLDEN CAT
The codes in the story reveal a tale of robberies and betrayals.
Here are the solutions, to help you piece together the events.

THE SOLUTIONS

Heruher was a greedy man. Being a foreman for the pharaoh Sematawy wasn't enough for him. He wanted power and riches. When the pharaoh died, he saw a chance to gain favor with the new pharaoh, Wermatre. He bribed his own workers to rob Sematawy's tomb. Then he caught them in the act at the tomb. He took some of the treasure, including one of the golden cats, but left its partner behind along with a piece of pottery showing the name of one of the tomb painters, Deduhapy. Then he went to Wermatre with the golden cat and the names of the robbers. The grateful pharaoh made him a royal seal bearer. Then Deduhapy and the other robbers were punished: Wermatre had their hands cut off. Now Heruher was rich and powerful enough to marry the pharaoh's own daughter, Hemira, and join the royal family. When Wermatre died, Heruher put the cat next to his tomb. But he fell into the Nile on the way home and drowned. Was it the cat's revenge? Hemira knew he was fond of the cat and bribed a priest to move it to her husband's tomb in the room next to his master, her father (Wermatre). She wanted him to know it was there but had to keep it a secret. So she wrote a message to him in the bowl that she used to leave offerings at the tomb, together with simple directions to get there in case she had to send a steward. When she died, she was buried in the tomb, and the slave kept using the bowl to carry offerings to her. It held the secret of the golden cat for 3,000 years.

THE ANSWERS TO THE EIGHT CODES:

• CODE ONE (page 14) The label reads: "Wall paintings in the tomb show two golden cats, but only one statue was found."

• CODE TWO (page 15) The note on the scroll reads: "We can find the golden cat together. Meet me in the museum garden."

• CODE THREE (page 20) The name of the pharaoh is S(E)M(A)TAWY.

• CODE FOUR (page 21) The name on the fragment of pottery is D(E)DUHAPY.

• CODE FIVE (page 25) Which pharaoh was Heruher writing letters to? The hieroglyphs spell out RE-W(E)RM(A)T. Once the god's name is put at the end, you get W(E)RM(A)TRE.

• CODE SIX (page 28) Wermatre punished the tomb robbers by cutting off their hands.

• EXTRA CHALLENGES (page 29) The punishments being shown are (left to right): 1) being tied up and imprisoned; 2) being beaten and taken prisoner in war; 3) having an ear cut off. The instrument shown on page 29, the cattle-branding iron, is similar to the branding irons that would be used to burn a mark onto a criminal so that everyone would know that person was a law breaker.

• CODE SEVEN (page 35) The ideograms on the bowl give the following directions: "From the city, go north along the river to a wall beside a hill where the tomb is." They were directions to a secret entrance to the tomb of Wermatre.

• CODE EIGHT (page 41) Nefret was the spirit of the lost Golden Cat. She came to life in human form to guide Dr. Stone to the lost tomb so that the two cats could be reunited.

Note: The detective story is fictional. None of the characters named above are real.